Messy Blessings

Yessing the Unloved,
the Unremarkable,
and the Uncute

Written by Jeff Williams
Illustrated by Madeline Barber

"Messy Blessings"
Text and illustrations copyright ©2021
By 320 Sycamore Studios.

All rights reserved.

No part of this book may be used or reproduced in any manner whatsoever without written permission with the exception of brief quotations intended for review.

For information, visit 320sycamorestudios.com.

ISBN: 978-1-7358041-4-9

First edition.

Page design by Robert Louis Henry.

www.320sycamorestudios.com

For my sister Tracie: Every kind of blessing.

— Jeff

To my parents (and biggest fans), Mitzi and Chuck Barber.

— Madeline

We "No" so much there's much not blessed

but don't you think it should be stressed
there's more in life that should be yessed?

Hey, let's put blessing to a test!

Bless rotten pumpkins.

Bless some bugs.

Bless awkward people's awkward hugs.

Bless those nettles. Bless this cactus.

Bless a booger just for practice.

Bless snot and phlegm and sneezing fits.

Bless you with all your stinky bits.

Bless ordinary blades of grass.

Bless any piece of broken glass.

Bless feeling sick and throwing up.
Bless feeling weird

and growing up.

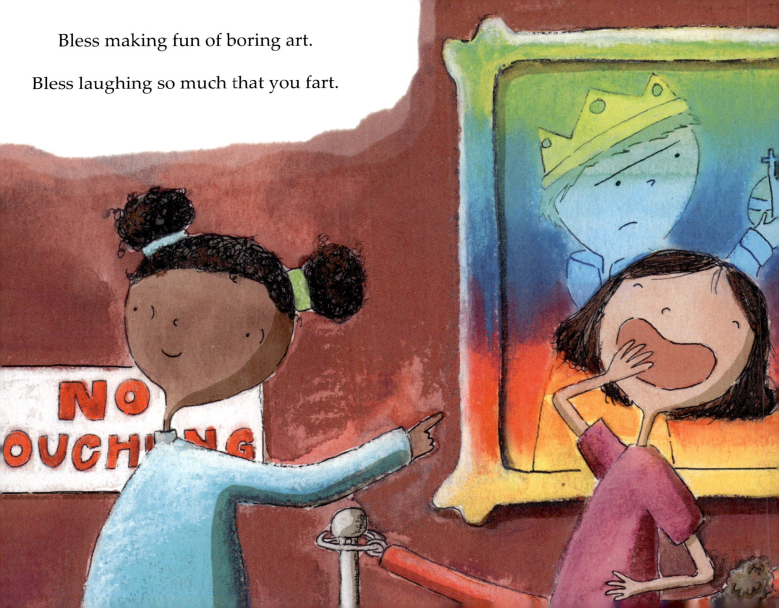

Bless making fun of boring art.

Bless laughing so much that you fart.

Bless grumpy people on the train.

Bless highway traffic in the rain.

Bless snakes that hide beneath the flowers.

Bless minutes fast becoming hours.

Bless all the people you forgot.

Bless nada, zilch, and diddly squat.

Bless mischief that you instigate.

And bless too little done too

late.

Bless U-less words that start with Q.
Bless chicken pox

and bless the flu.

Bless good and bad and all the rest.

'Cause good or bad, life's better blessed.

Now, look around at all you've yessed

and count your blessings, kid.

And rest.

The End.

Looking for your next great-read aloud book?

In this overbusy world, we make it easy for families
to slow down and connect. Each week we send out our big-hearted, irreverent, smartly
crafted stories — for free — the kind of stories you can't wait to read together.

Get a story in your inbox every week.
Visit 320sycamorestudios.com to find out more.

Happy reading!

www.320sycamorestudios.com

Made in the USA
Middletown, DE
28 September 2021

49267312R00015